SCHOOL LIBRARY MEDIA SERIES
Edited by Diane de Cordova Biesel

1. *Chalk Talk Stories,* written and illustrated by Arden Druce, 1993.
2. *Toddler Storytime Programs,* by Diane Briggs, 1993.
3. *Alphabet: A Handbook of ABC Books and Book Extensions for the Elementary Classroom, second edition,* by Patricia L. Roberts, 1994.
4. *Cultural Cobblestones: Teaching Cultural Diversity,* by Lynda Miller, Theresa Steinlage, and Mike Printz, 1994.
5. *ABC Books and Activities: From Preschool to High School,* by Cathie Hilterbran Cooper, 1996.
6. *ZOOLUTIONS: A Mathematical Expedition with Topics for Grades 4 through 8,* by Anne Burgunder and Vaunda Nelson, 1996.
7. *Library Lessons for Grades 7–9,* by Arden Druce, 1997.
8. *Counting your Way through 1-2-3 Books and Activities,* by Cathie Hilterbran Cooper, 1997.
9. *Art and Children: Using Literature to Expand Creativity,* by Robin W. Davis, 1996.
10. *Story Programs: A Source Book of Materials, second edition,* by Carolyn Sue Peterson and Ann Fenton, 1997.
11. *Taking Humor Seriously in Children's Literature: Literature-Based Mini-Units and Humorous Books for Children Ages 5–12,* by Patricia L. Roberts, 1997.
12. *Multicultural Friendship Stories and Activities for Children, Ages 5–14,* by Patricia L. Roberts, 1997.
13. *Side by Side: Twelve Multicultural Puppet Plays,* by Jean M. Pollock, 1997.
14. *Reading Fun: Quick and Easy Activities for the School Library Media Center,* by Mona Kerby, 1998.
15. *Paper Bag Puppets,* by Arden Druce with illustrations by Geraldine Hulbert, Cynthia Johnson, Harvey H. Lively, and Carol Ditter Waters, 1998.

Reading Fun

Quick and Easy Activities for the School Library Media Center

Mona Kerby

School Library Media Series, No. 14

The Scarecrow Press, Inc.
Lanham, Md., & London
1998

SCARECROW PRESS, INC.

Published in the United States of America
by Scarecrow Press, Inc.
4720 Boston Way
Lanham, Maryland 20706

British Library Cataloguing in Publication Information available

Library of Congress Cataloging-in-Publication Data

Kerby, Mona.
    Reading fun : quick and easy activities for the school library media center / Mona Kerby.
      p.   cm. — (School library media series ; no. 14)
    Includes bibliographical references.
    ISBN 0-8108-3361-1 (paper : alk. paper)
    1. Elementary school libraries—Activity programs—United States.   I. Title.   II. Series.
    Z675.S3K46   1998
    027.62′5—dc21
                                          97-21445
                                                CIP

ISBN 0-8108-3361-1 (pbk. : alk. paper)

For Sue Rose, Shirley Scott,
and the school library media specialists in Arlington, Texas.

For my students at Western Maryland College.

And most especially, for young students everywhere
who enjoying reading books.

CONTENTS

EDITOR'S FOREWORD

The School Library Media Series is directed to the school library media specialist, particularly the building level librarian. The multifaceted role of the librarian as educator, collection developer, curriculum developer, and information specialist is examined. The series includes concise, practical books on topical and current subjects related to programs and services.

Reading Fun is just that—fun to read and fun to do. Dr. Kerby has been in the trenches and has produced homemade activities and homemade designs that will be very helpful for the harried and hurried school librarian. Everything from a bird whistling contest (which she did once) to Newbery Bingo is presented with delightfully helpful hints. This book will definitely make your life easier.

Diane de Cordova Biesel
Series Editor

PREFACE

This book is designed to promote the enjoyment of reading in the elementary school.

We school library media specialists wear many hats. According to *Information Power,* we are informational specialists, teachers, and instructional consultants. We must know books, technology, how to find and use information, and we must know our students and their individual learning needs. We not only work cooperatively with the faculty, we also integrate library media lessons with the curriculum by using a variety of teaching strategies. We have an extraordinary, exhilarating, and sometimes exhausting job.

One of our stated missions is to ensure that students are effective users of ideas and information. One way to accomplish this is to stimulate interest in reading. Unfortunately, however, encouraging students to read for pleasure often takes a back seat to skills. Yet the joy of reading is at the heart of using information, and it is at the heart of becoming a lifelong learner.

Reading Fun: Quick and Easy Activities for the School Library Media Center will motivate your students to read. At the beginning of each unit, I've included some basic suggestions for using the activities, but there are plenty of opportunities for you to mold these activities to fit your own special needs. Don't be fooled by the simplicity of these ideas. The activities are simple AND they work.

For fifteen years, I served as the school library media specialist at J. B. Little Elementary School in the Arlington (Texas) Independent School District. The ideas in this book are some of my students' favorite reading activities. Some are not original. Our school district "borrowed" the Caldecott Reading Diary from another district, which then became my pattern for the Newbery Diary and the Beverly Cleary Diary. Calico Cat was adapted from the Texas Education Agency's *Attracting Students and Teachers to the Library Media Center.*

Every fall, I used to serve pizza to the kids who completed the summer reading calendar. Every spring on awards day, I awarded the hardworking independent scholars with certificates and library pens purchased from one of the library vendors. We did the Bird Whistling Contest only once—I figured that a woman my age could only stand so much fun. But we still laugh about our star whistlers. That year, during rainy day recesses, the bird whistling video was a hit.

When working as a library media specialist, I raced through the day. My original sheets were plain. I would dream up the idea, type it up, copy it, race back to class just before the students arrived, and in the moments it took for the class to sit down, I would check in some books, say hello to the teacher, and answer a student's question. Sound familiar?

Here, I've taken the original ideas and redesigned them with Print Shop, Microsoft Publisher, Microsoft Word, and Corel Gallery. To save paper, some worksheets are printed twice on the same page because I suspect you probably run low on paper in your school as we sometimes did in ours. You will want to duplicate the Caldecott and Newbery games on card stock and laminate them so that you can use them for several years.

An artist with no clue about school library media centers did not design the activity sheets. These activities look homemade because they are. I designed them especially for you—as one school library media specialist to another. Like a handmade sweater knitted by a friend, this book is my gift to you.

More than once as I worked on this book, I wished that I had had these sheets to use with my own young students. May the activities save you precious time and be exactly what you need. And may you and your students have fun with books and reading.

INTRODUCTION

If you're going to motivate students to read, you need plenty of new and attractive books. There's nothing worse than giving an inspirational lesson and watching the students race to the shelves only to see them turn away at the sight of old, tattered books. Make no mistake—good lessons, your own personality, and attractive book collections are key factors in motivating students to read.

Look at your collection and weed. Buy some new titles, and put some shiny new covers on some of the books you already have.

Also, label your shelves. It's an effective way to encourage your students to read a variety of books and to help them become independent. Label every shelf in the fiction and easy sections with the corresponding alphabet letter. Label the sections of popular authors with their last names. Label the nonfiction shelves with Dewey numbers and subjects.

While you can order fancy labels from one of the library supply companies, many are difficult to see at a distance. Instead, select a large font on your word processor, and make your own. Use black ink and white paper. Attach them to the shelf with a wide piece of clear tape.

To verify that students did the reading for the different activities, I usually included a place on the worksheet for the student and also the parent to sign. I didn't require oral or written reports because I wanted the activity focused on reading.

When I doubted that a student actually did the reading—sometimes students signed for their parents—we had a quick, private chat. I mentioned trust, honesty, and an opportunity to try again.

Simple motivational strategies include posting readers' names in the school newspaper or having names read at morning announcements. Certificates are usually good with the younger students. A free 100 coupon motivates older students. Work out an arrangement with the language arts teachers so older students can use their 100 coupon as one language arts grade.

Whatever the lesson, I always gave students plenty of silent reading time. They had assigned seats. I told them that they were surrounded by some of the finest minds in the world—theirs and the authors'. I let them know that they could read or daydream, for both were important to an intellectual life. Get comfortable, I'd say. While you read and think, I will see that no one disturbs you.

The ideas in this book work best when practiced in moderation. Do not let the activity or the reward assume more importance than the act of reading. You don't always have to pass out a bookmark or present a showy lesson.

The pleasure of reading is its own reward. And if you've allowed your students plenty of silent reading time, they will know that truth.

CHAPTER 1

ANIMALS

In this section, you'll find two activities that you can use with the entire school and two for specific grade levels.

"Read Four Animal Books" works well with second graders. Animal crackers are an easy treat. Most students don't need much outside motivation to read animal books.

"Calico Cat" works with third graders. Copy the Calico Cat and the Reading Diary back-to-back on one piece of paper. When students finish reading, coloring, and filling in their ten titles, present them with the Calico Cat Reader certificate.

For the bird whistling activity, you'll want a bird book with a cassette of actual bird songs. I copied a few bird songs and then made a set of cassettes for temporary check-out. Have the students turn in their entry form early, so you'll know how many to expect. (I had fifteen entries out of 700 students.) When you video tape it, don't rehearse. Film it quickly. The video will be hilarious and a hit at PTA meetings and rainy day recess.

When we did the insect contest, we had a hundred insects in the library media center. We tried to recognize every creature—the smallest, the largest, the ugliest, etc.

My guess is you'll do the bird whistling and insect contests just once. If you do either activity *two* years in a row, I want to meet you.

Read 4 Animal Books and Eat a Treat!

Read four animal books from the nonfiction section of the library media center between now and _____, and earn a small sweet treat. Hooray for books and treats!

_____
School Library Media Specialist

I read these books:

1. _____

2. _____

3. _____

4. _____

_____   _____
Student Signature   *Parent Signature*

_____

Read 4 Animal Books and Eat a Treat!

Read four animal books from the nonfiction section of the library media center between now and _____, and earn a small sweet treat. Hooray for books and treats!

_____
School Library Media Specialist

I read these books:

1. _____

2. _____

3. _____

4. _____

_____   _____
Student Signature   *Parent Signature*

Calico Cat Reading Diary

Here's your chance to explore the school library media center and read a variety of books! Read a book from these sections of the media center, list the title and then color the patch on Calico Cat. That's all it takes to earn a *Calico Cat Reader Certificate*.

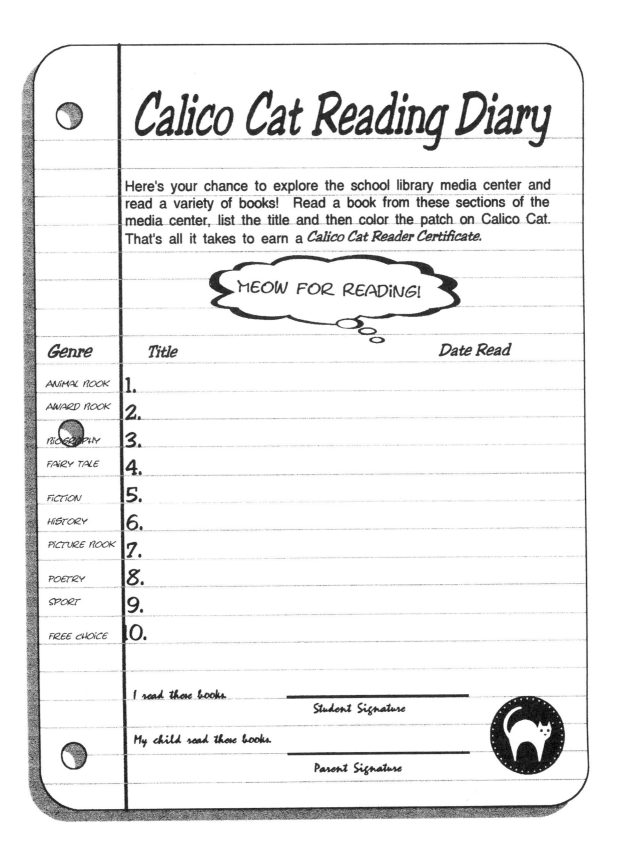

MEOW FOR READING!

Genre	Title	Date Read
ANIMAL BOOK	1.	
AWARD BOOK	2.	
BIOGRAPHY	3.	
FAIRY TALE	4.	
FICTION	5.	
HISTORY	6.	
PICTURE BOOK	7.	
POETRY	8.	
SPORT	9.	
FREE CHOICE	10.	

I read these books.
_____
Student Signature

My child read these books.
_____
Parent Signature

Calico Cat

Calico Cat Reader Certificate

_____

Has Earned This Award by
Reading a Variety of Library Books

Congratulations!

_____
Library Media Specialist

_____
School

_____
Date

Whistle a bird song and be a star!

That's right. _____ will be Bird Whistling Day in the school library media center. Whistlers will receive a certificate and also star in a video. Don't miss out on this once-in-a-lifetime opportunity. Cheers for books and birds!

Official Bird Whistling Rules

1. Identify your bird and state some facts about it. Check out a bird book from the 598 section of the media center or look up your bird in the reference materials.

2. Know your bird's call. You may want to check out a cassette tape of bird songs. Or, you may just want to sit under a tree and listen.

3. Your entire presentation should last less than one minute.

4. Complete the entry form and return it to the library media center by _____

Official Bird Whistling Entry Form

Student Name:

Date:

Name of Bird:

Name of the book or reference materials you used:

Describe your bird. Then state one interesting fact you learned.

Tweet *Tweet*

Bird Whistler Award

TO

_____

For Whistling a Bird Song in the Library Media Center

_____
Library Media Specialist

_____
School

_____
Date

Insect Delight

Bring Your Favorite Insect to School!

When was the last time you read a good book on bugs? When was the last time you invited a bug to school? Celebrate Insect Day in the Library Media Center. Bring an insect to school on _____ and earn an award. Don't miss out on Insect Delight!

To enter the Insect Contest, follow these rules:

1. Read a book on insects. Check the 595 section of the library media center.

2. On Insect Day, bring your pal in a cage. Find information on cages in the media center.

3. Your insect must be alive.

4. Attach the completed entry form to the cage.

5. At the end of Insect Day, stop by the library media center and pick up your pal.

- - - - - - - - - - - - - - - - - - - -

Official Insect Entry Form

Common name of insect:

Scientific name of insect:

Name the book you read:

State one interesting fact about your insect:

Student Name: _____

Teacher's Name: _____ Grade Level: _____

Insect Award

To

_____

For Participating in the Library Media Center Insect Contest

Your Insect

_____

Has Hereby Been Declared

_____

Here's to Bugs!

_____
Library Media Specialist

_____
School

_____
Date

CHAPTER 2

AUTHORS FOR PRIMARY STUDENTS

In our district, we followed a curriculum guide we had written that included goals, objectives, and activities for each grade level. More than likely, your district has developed its own curriculum guide to meet the needs of your students. To my way of thinking, the two major goals for students in kindergarten, first, and second grades are: (1) to recognize books, authors, and illustrators, and (2) to know how to find books.

Spend several weeks on one author. Point out the shelf location for the author, and in subsequent weeks, have students point out the shelf. As the class leaves the media center, have each child tell you the author's name, and something he/she has written. I used to tell them to teach their parents what they learned in the library (we called our media center by its lovely, old-fashioned name) and to be very patient with their parents if they weren't "book smart" like they were. As a reminder, I made bookmarks on a variety of authors, including Marc Brown, Ezra Jack Keats, James Marshall, Patricia McKissack, Bill Peet, and Patricia Polacco.

A couple of the publishing companies used to send author cards for reading incentives. It's great if you can get them, but if you can't, here are reading activities and author cards for Joanna Cole, Patricia Reilly Giff, and Arnold Lobel. Notice that the Joanna Cole and the Pat Giff cards are autographed on the back.

Marc Brown

Today, in the school library media center, we studied books by

Marc Brown

(On the back, list some of his titles.)

Marc Brown

Today, in the school library media center, we studied books by

Marc Brown

(On the back, list some of his titles.)

Marc Brown

Today, in the school library media center, we studied books by

Marc Brown

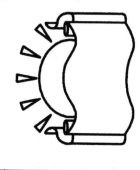

(On the back, list some of his titles.)

Marc Brown

Today, in the school library media center, we studied books by

Marc Brown

(On the back, list some of his titles.)

Ezra Jack Keats

Today, in the school library media center, we studied books by

Ezra Jack Keats

(On the back, list some of his titles.)

Ezra Jack Keats

Today, in the school library media center, we studied books by

Ezra Jack Keats

(On the back, list some of his titles.)

Ezra Jack Keats

Today, in the school library media center, we studied books by

Ezra Jack Keats

(On the back, list some of his titles.)

Ezra Jack Keats

Today, in the school library media center, we studied books by

Ezra Jack Keats

(On the back, list some of his titles.)

James Marshall

Today, in the school library media center, we studied books by

James Marshall

(On the back, list some of his titles.)

James Marshall

Today, in the school library media center, we studied books by

James Marshall

(On the back, list some of his titles.)

James Marshall

Today, in the school library media center, we studied books by

James Marshall

(On the back, list some of his titles.)

James Marshall

Today, in the school library media center, we studied books by

James Marshall

(On the back, list some of his titles.)

Patricia McKissack

Today, in the school library media center, we studied books by

Patricia McKissack

(On the back, list some of her titles.)

Patricia McKissack

Today, in the school library media center, we studied books by

Patricia McKissack

(On the back, list some of her titles.)

Patricia McKissack

Today, in the school library media center, we studied books by

Patricia McKissack

(On the back, list some of her titles.)

Patricia McKissack

Today, in the school library media center, we studied books by

Patricia McKissack

(On the back, list some of her titles.)

Bill Peet

Today, in the school library media center, we studied books by

Bill Peet

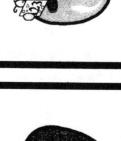

(On the back, list some of his titles.)

Bill Peet

Today, in the school library media center, we studied books by

Bill Peet

(On the back, list some of his titles.)

Bill Peet

Today, in the school library media center, we studied books by

Bill Peet

(On the back, list some of his titles.)

Bill Peet

Today, in the school library media center, we studied books by

Bill Peet

(On the back, list some of his titles.)

Patricia Polacco

Today, in the school library media center, we studied books by

Patricia Polacco

(On the back, list some of her titles.)

Patricia Polacco

Today, in the school library media center, we studied books by

Patricia Polacco

(On the back, list some of her titles.)

Patricia Polacco

Today, in the school library media center, we studied books by

Patricia Polacco

(On the back, list some of her titles.)

Patricia Polacco

Today, in the school library media center, we studied books by

Patricia Polacco

(On the back, list some of her titles.)

Read 4 Joanna Cole Books & Earn a Cole Card

Joanna Cole has written a variety of books. Read four of her titles between now and _____, and add another author card to your collection. Check out a Joanna Cole book today!

_____
School Library Media Specialist

I read these books:

1. _____

2. _____

3. _____

4. _____

_____
Student Signature

_____
Parent   Signature

Read 4 Joanna Cole Books & Earn a Cole Card

Joanna Cole has written a variety of books. Read four of her titles between now and _____, and add another author card to your collection. Check out a Joanna Cole book today!

_____
School Library Media Specialist

I read these books:

1. _____

2. _____

3. _____

4. _____

_____
Student Signature

_____
Parent   Signature

Joanna Cole Card

_____

This outstanding student is a reader of
Joanna Cole books and is hereby recognized
by the school library media center.

Joanna Cole Card

_____

This outstanding student is a reader of
Joanna Cole books and is hereby recognized
by the school library media center.

Joanna Cole Card

_____

This outstanding student is a reader of
Joanna Cole books and is hereby recognized
by the school library media center.

Joanna Cole Card

_____

This outstanding student is a reader of
Joanna Cole books and is hereby recognized
by the school library media center.

Joanna Cole Card

_____

This outstanding student is a reader of
Joanna Cole books and is hereby recognized
by the school library media center.

Joanna Cole Card

_____

This outstanding student is a reader of
Joanna Cole books and is hereby recognized
by the school library media center.

Joanna Cole Card

_____

This outstanding student is a reader of
Joanna Cole books and is hereby recognized
by the school library media center.

Joanna Cole Card

_____

This outstanding student is a reader of
Joanna Cole books and is hereby recognized
by the school library media center.

Author Autograph:

Joanna Cole

Author Autograph:

Joanna Cole

Author Autograph:

Joanna Cole

Author Autograph:

Joanna Cole

Author Autograph:

Joanna Cole

Author Autograph:

Joanna Cole

Author Autograph:

Joanna Cole

Author Autograph:

Joanna Cole

Read 3 Patricia Reilly Giff Books & Earn a Giff Card

Earn a Patricia Reilly Giff card for your author collection! Read three of her books between now and _____. You can read books from our library media center or from the public library. Yea, books!

_____
School Library Media Specialist

I read these books:

1. _____

2. _____

3. _____

_____   _____
Student Signature   Parent Signature

Read 3 Patricia Reilly Giff Books & Earn a Giff Card

Earn a Patricia Reilly Giff card for your author collection! Read three of her books between now and _____. You can read books from our library media center or from the public library. Yea, books!

_____
School Library Media Specialist

I read these books:

1. _____

2. _____

3. _____

_____   _____
Student Signature   Parent Signature

Patricia Reilly Giff Card

_____

This outstanding student is a reader of Patricia Reilly Giff books and is hereby recognized by the school library media center.

Patricia Reilly Giff Card

_____

This outstanding student is a reader of Patricia Reilly Giff books and is hereby recognized by the school library media center.

Patricia Reilly Giff Card

_____

This outstanding student is a reader of Patricia Reilly Giff books and is hereby recognized by the school library media center.

Patricia Reilly Giff Card

_____

This outstanding student is a reader of Patricia Reilly Giff books and is hereby recognized by the school library media center.

Patricia Reilly Giff Card

_____

This outstanding student is a reader of Patricia Reilly Giff books and is hereby recognized by the school library media center.

Patricia Reilly Giff Card

_____

This outstanding student is a reader of Patricia Reilly Giff books and is hereby recognized by the school library media center.

Patricia Reilly Giff Card

_____

This outstanding student is a reader of Patricia Reilly Giff books and is hereby recognized by the school library media center.

Patricia Reilly Giff Card

_____

This outstanding student is a reader of Patricia Reilly Giff books and is hereby recognized by the school library media center.

Author Autograph:

Patricia Reilly Giff

Author Autograph:

Patricia Reilly Giff

Author Autograph:

Patricia Reilly Giff

Author Autograph:

Patricia Reilly Giff

Author Autograph:

Patricia Reilly Giff

Author Autograph:

Patricia Reilly Giff

Author Autograph:

Patricia Reilly Giff

Author Autograph:

Patricia Reilly Giff

Read 4 Arnold Lobel Books & Earn a Lobel Card

Here's your chance to earn a Lobel card for your pocket. All you have to do is read four books by Arnold Lobel between now and _____. You can read books from our library media center or from the public library. Join the fun and start reading today!

_____
School Library Media Specialist

I read these books:

1. _____

2. _____

3. _____

4. _____

Look for Frog & Toad books!

_____
Student Signature

_____
Parent Signature

_____

Read 4 Arnold Lobel Books & Earn a Lobel Card

Here's your chance to earn a Lobel card for your pocket. All you have to do is read four books by Arnold Lobel between now and _____. You can read books from our library media center or from the public library. Join the fun and start reading today!

_____
School Library Media Specialist

I read these books:

1. _____

2. _____

3. _____

4. _____

Look for Frog & Toad books!

_____
Student Signature

_____
Parent Signature

Arnold Lobel Card

_____

This outstanding student is a reader of Arnold Lobel books and is hereby recognized by the school library media center.

Arnold Lobel Card

_____

This outstanding student is a reader of Arnold Lobel books and is hereby recognized by the school library media center.

Arnold Lobel Card

_____

This outstanding student is a reader of Arnold Lobel books and is hereby recognized by the school library media center.

Arnold Lobel Card

_____

This outstanding student is a reader of Arnold Lobel books and is hereby recognized by the school library media center.

Arnold Lobel Card

_____

This outstanding student is a reader of Arnold Lobel books and is hereby recognized by the school library media center.

Arnold Lobel Card

_____

This outstanding student is a reader of Arnold Lobel books and is hereby recognized by the school library media center.

Arnold Lobel Card

_____

This outstanding student is a reader of Arnold Lobel books and is hereby recognized by the school library media center.

Arnold Lobel Card

_____

This outstanding student is a reader of Arnold Lobel books and is hereby recognized by the school library media center.

CHAPTER 3

MORE ACTIVITIES FOR PRIMARY STUDENTS

When little children have a hard time sitting still, get them up on their feet. With these three activities, they'll be having fun and learning, too.

Use "Easy Fiction Shelves" as a follow-up for your presentation on how easy fiction books are arranged. Before class, tag your shelves with the symbols that appear on the worksheets. (Remove them after the activity.) Tell your students that they are to find the different shelves, not memorize the symbols. To avoid a stampede at the "A" shelf, have some students start in the middle and at the end of the shelves. Some might check out their books first.

For "Cheers for Me," have the class sit in front of the easy fiction (or nonfiction) section and let each child practice finding a shelf. Say, "Touch the 'B' shelf" and then hesitate a few seconds before you call on someone. The hesitation is so that all the students will be looking for the answer, thinking that you might call on them. By the time you do this activity with every kindergarten, first, and second grade class, you'll be feeling a little frazzled.

If you would like to share some of this "cheer" with others, use student tutors. Older students can check the younger ones, and everybody learns in the process.

I used the Mother Goose Award after I read nursery rhymes to the kindergarten students. Students stood close beside me and in front of their classmates and recited a rhyme. Be sure to point out the Mother Goose shelf in the nonfiction section. Never make the nonfiction section off limits to the younger students.

Name _____ Date _____

Easy Fiction Shelves

Find the following easy fiction shelves. Copy down the symbols that you see taped on the shelves.

E
B _____

E
G _____

E
L _____

E
P _____

E
R _____

E
W _____

_____

Name _____ Date _____

Easy Fiction Shelves

Find the following easy fiction shelves. Copy down the symbols that you see taped on the shelves.

E
B _____

E
G _____

E
L _____

E
P _____

E
R _____

E
W _____

Cheers for ME!

Today, in the school library media center, I found these shelves:

BRAVO!

Cheers for ME!

Today, in the school library media center, I found these shelves:

BRAVO!

Cheers for ME!

Today, in the school library media center, I found these shelves:

BRAVO!

Cheers for ME!

Today, in the school library media center, I found these shelves:

BRAVO!

Congratulations

To

_____

For Reciting a Mother Goose Rhyme in the Library Media Center

| Library Media Specialist | School | Date |

CHAPTER 4

AUTHORS FOR INTERMEDIATE STUDENTS

I introduced Beverly Cleary's books to the third graders, Bill Wallace's to the fourth graders, and Betsy Byars's to the fifth graders. I usually had three or four lessons on each author. For the first lesson, I'd tell something about the author's life, display and talk about some of his/her titles, and then hand out the reading diary. For other lessons, I'd show a video of the author, read passages from the books, or have the students perform Reader's Theater. (See Caroline Feller Bauer's book *Presenting Reader's Theater: Plays and Poems to Read Aloud* published by Wilson in 1987.) I encouraged, but never demanded that students check out the books we were discussing.

Notice that the fourth and fifth graders earn a free 100 coupon instead of receiving a certificate. See if the language arts teachers will count it as a language arts grade.

In this section, I've included Seymour Simon and Jean Fritz cards. Both authors sent their autographs, which can be duplicated on the back of the cards. I've also included bookmarks for Johanna Hurwitz, Barbara Park, and Gary Paulsen. For all of these authors, you will want to prepare a bibliography of the books that you have in your collection.

Beverly Cleary Books

Dear Students,

We will be studying the books written by Beverly Cleary. Both the school library media center and the public library have many of her books.

If you read three of her books between now and _____, you will receive a Beverly Cleary Reader Certificate.

Just complete these steps: (1) read, (2) discuss the books with your parents, and (3) return this form to the media center. Happy reading!

Sincerely,

Library Media Specialist

I read these books:

1. _____

2. _____

3. _____

_____
Student Signature

_____
Parent Signature

34

Beverly Cleary Books

Dear Students,

We will be studying the books written by Beverly Cleary. Both the school library media center and the public library have many of her books.

If you read three of her books between now and _____, you will receive a Beverly Cleary Reader Certificate.

Just complete these steps: (1) read, (2) discuss the books with your parents, and (3) return this form to the media center. Happy reading!

Sincerely,

Library Media Specialist

I read these books:

1. _____

2. _____

3. _____

_____
Student Signature

_____
Parent Signature

Beverly Cleary

Reader Certificate

Awarded To

_____

For Reading Beverly Cleary Books

_____
Library Media Specialist

_____
School

_____
Date

Bill Wallace Books

If you read one Bill Wallace book between now and _____, you'll earn a free 100 coupon that you may use in language arts class. When you finish reading, complete this form, and return it to the library media center.

Title of book :

Name two characters in this book :

What was the most exciting part?

I read this book. (Student) _____

I saw my student read this book. (Teacher) _____

- -

Bill Wallace Books

If you read one Bill Wallace book between now and _____, you'll earn a free 100 coupon that you may use in language arts class. When you finish reading, complete this form, and return it to the library media center.

Title of book :

Name two characters in this book :

What was the most exciting part?

I read this book. (Student) _____

I saw my student read this book. (Teacher) _____

Betsy Byars Books

If you read two Betsy Byars books between now and _____,
you'll earn a free 100 coupon that you may use in language arts class. Just
complete this form and return it to the school library media center.

Title of Book:

1. _____

2. _____

I read these books. (Student) _____

I saw my student read these books. (Teacher) _____

Betsy Byars Books

If you read two Betsy Byars books between now and _____,
you'll earn a free 100 coupon that you may use in language arts class. Just
complete this form and return it to the school library media center.

Title of Book:

1. _____

2. _____

I read these books. (Student) _____

I saw my student read these books. (Teacher) _____

Free 100 Coupon!

Congratulations To:

_____

You have earned a free 100 because you are such a dedicated reader. Check with your teacher to see how you can use this coupon.

Great!

_____
Library Media Specialist

_____
Date

Free 100 Coupon!

Congratulations To:

_____

You have earned a free 100 because you are such a dedicated reader. Check with your teacher to see how you can use this coupon.

Great!

_____
Library Media Specialist

_____
Date

Read 3 Jean Fritz Books and Earn a Fritz Card

Read three Jean Fritz books between now and _____, and you'll
earn an autographed author card. It even counts if your parents read to you. Start today!

_____
School Library Media Specialist

I read these books:

1. _____

2. _____

3. _____

_____   _____
Student Signature   Parent Signature

Read 3 Jean Fritz Books and Earn a Fritz Card

Read three Jean Fritz books between now and _____, and you'll
earn an autographed author card. It even counts if your parents read to you. Start today!

_____
School Library Media Specialist

I read these books:

1. _____

2. _____

3. _____

_____   _____
Student Signature   Parent Signature

Jean Fritz Card

_____

This outstanding student is a reader of
Jean Fritz books and is hereby recognized
by the school library media center.

Jean Fritz Card

_____

This outstanding student is a reader of
Jean Fritz books and is hereby recognized
by the school library media center.

Jean Fritz Card

_____

This outstanding student is a reader of
Jean Fritz books and is hereby recognized
by the school library media center.

Jean Fritz Card

_____

This outstanding student is a reader of
Jean Fritz books and is hereby recognized
by the school library media center.

Jean Fritz Card

_____

This outstanding student is a reader of
Jean Fritz books and is hereby recognized
by the school library media center.

Jean Fritz Card

_____

This outstanding student is a reader of
Jean Fritz books and is hereby recognized
by the school library media center.

Jean Fritz Card

_____

This outstanding student is a reader of
Jean Fritz books and is hereby recognized
by the school library media center.

Jean Fritz Card

_____

This outstanding student is a reader of
Jean Fritz books and is hereby recognized
by the school library media center.

Author Autograph:

Jean Fritz

Author Autograph:

Jean Fritz

Author Autograph:

Jean Fritz

Author Autograph:

Jean Fritz

Author Autograph:

Jean Fritz

Author Autograph:

Jean Fritz

Author Autograph:

Jean Fritz

Author Autograph:

Jean Fritz

READ 3 SEYMOUR SIMON BOOKS AND EARN A SIMON CARD

Read three Seymour Simon books between now and _____, and you'll earn an autographed author card. It even counts if your parents read to you. Cheers for books!

_____
School Library Media Specialist

I READ THESE BOOKS:

1. _____

2. _____

3. _____

_____
Student Signature

_____
Parent Signature

READ 3 SEYMOUR SIMON BOOKS AND EARN A SIMON CARD

Read three Seymour Simon books between now and _____, and you'll earn an autographed author card. It even counts if your parents read to you. Cheers for books!

_____
School Library Media Specialist

I READ THESE BOOKS:

1. _____

2. _____

3. _____

_____
Student Signature

_____
Parent Signature

Seymour Simon Card

_____

This outstanding student is a reader of
Seymour Simon books & is hereby recognized
by the school library media center.

Seymour Simon Card

_____

This outstanding student is a reader of
Seymour Simon books & is hereby recognized
by the school library media center.

Seymour Simon Card

_____

This outstanding student is a reader of
Seymour Simon books & is hereby recognized
by the school library media center.

Seymour Simon Card

_____

This outstanding student is a reader of
Seymour Simon books & is hereby recognized
by the school library media center.

Seymour Simon Card

_____

This outstanding student is a reader of
Seymour Simon books & is hereby recognized
by the school library media center.

Seymour Simon Card

_____

This outstanding student is a reader of
Seymour Simon books & is hereby recognized
by the school library media center.

Seymour Simon Card

_____

This outstanding student is a reader of
Seymour Simon books & is hereby recognized
by the school library media center.

Seymour Simon Card

_____

This outstanding student is a reader of
Seymour Simon books & is hereby recognized
by the school library media center.

Author Autograph:

Seymour Simon

Author Autograph:

Seymour Simon

Author Autograph:

Seymour Simon

Author Autograph:

Seymour Simon

Author Autograph:

Seymour Simon

Author Autograph:

Seymour Simon

Author Autograph:

Seymour Simon

Author Autograph:

Seymour Simon

Johanna Hurwitz

Today, in the school library media center, we studied books by

Johanna Hurwitz

(On the back, list some of her titles.)

Johanna Hurwitz

Today, in the school library media center, we studied books by

Johanna Hurwitz

(On the back, list some of her titles.)

Johanna Hurwitz

Today, in the school library media center, we studied books by

Johanna Hurwitz

(On the back, list some of her titles.)

Johanna Hurwitz

Today, in the school library media center, we studied books by

Johanna Hurwitz

(On the back, list some of her titles.)

Barbara Park

Barbara Park

Today, in the school library media center, we studied books by

Barbara Park

(On the back, list some of her books.)

Barbara Park

Today, in the school library media center, we studied books by

Barbara Park

(On the back, list some of her books.)

Barbara Park

Today, in the school library media center, we studied books by

Barbara Park

(On the back, list some of her books.)

Barbara Park

Today, in the school library media center, we studied books by

Barbara Park

(On the back, list some of her books.)

Gary Paulsen

Today, in the school library media center, we studied books by

Gary Paulsen

(On the back, list some of his titles.)

Gary Paulsen

Today, in the school library media center, we studied books by

Gary Paulsen

(On the back, list some of his titles.)

Gary Paulsen

Today, in the school library media center, we studied books by

Gary Paulsen

(On the back, list some of his titles.)

Gary Paulsen

Today, in the school library media center, we studied books by

Gary Paulsen

(On the back, list some of his titles.)

CHAPTER 5

BIBLIOGRAPHIES

When we began a new author/illustrator study unit, I usually typed a half-sized-sheet bibliography of the books by that author/illustrator. This is an example of what I put at the bottom of the bibliography: "For more books written by Bill Peet, look in the catalog under Peet. When you visit the public library, look for the books written by him."

When new books arrived, I did quick talks on about fifteen titles. I then dismissed the students to their assigned seats, where they found new books spread out on the tables. For several minutes, they examined these books and made notes of titles that interested them. Then, I called time and students rotated to the next table. I repeated this until they had a chance to look at everything.

At other times, I let the students make up their own bibliographies. One, I wanted them to learn how to prepare a simple bibliography and even more importantly, I wanted them to explore all sections of the library. I would send the class to the shelves—only one student to a three-foot section—telling the students to pick a section that they didn't know. "Sit on the floor, away from your friends," I'd say, "and in five minutes, I'll call time, and you can go to a new section." You can also have them bring their chairs to the shelves.

In this activity, students of all abilities can stay on task and feel successful, as they take charge of their learning. This quiet activity can be repeated throughout the year.

The following bibliographies give you a variety of options, depending on time and student ability. You'll see that there aren't many lines for writing. I found that when I made longer worksheets, students spent too much time writing, which defeated my purpose of letting them read.

Name _____ Date _____

Hooray For New Books!

Take a look at the new books we have in the school library media center. When you find some good ones, list the title, the computer code, and the call number. Keep your bibliography; in the next few weeks you may want to check out something new!

    computer code   *title of the book*   *call number*

1. _____

2. _____

3. _____

4. _____

5. _____

Name _____ Date _____

Hooray For New Books!

Take a look at the new books we have in the school library media center. When you find some good ones, list the title, the computer code, and the call number. Keep your bibliography; in the next few weeks you may want to check out something new!

    computer code   *title of the book*   *call number*

1. _____

2. _____

3. _____

4. _____

5. _____

Name _____ Date _____

A BIBLIOGRAPHY OF BOOKS I WANT TO READ

Select one section of books and look at them. Read the inside covers and the first few pages. When you find a good book, write the author's last name, the title, and the call number. The next time you're in the school library media center, use your own personalized bibliography!

author's last name   *title of the book*   *call number*

1. _____

2. _____

3. _____

4. _____

5. _____

6. _____

Name _____ Date _____

A BIBLIOGRAPHY OF BOOKS I WANT TO READ

Select one section of books and look at them. Read the inside covers and the first few pages. When you find a good book, write the author's last name, the title, and the call number. The next time you're in the school library media center, use your own personalized bibliography!

author's last name   *title of the book*   *call number*

1. _____

2. _____

3. _____

4. _____

5. _____

6. _____

Name _____ Date _____

A HUNT FOR HiDDEN TREASURE

Explore the hidden treasure in the school library media center. Pick one section of shelves in the following areas. Examine the books by looking at the covers and by reading a few pages. Take good notes for your personal treasure map!

Author's last name	*Title*	*Call Number*

EASY FiCTiON

1. _____

2. _____

3. _____

FiCTiON

1. _____

2. _____

3. _____

NONFiCTiON

1. _____

2. _____

3. _____

CHAPTER 6

BIOGRAPHY BOOKS

"Join the Biography Reader's Club and Have Lunch with Santa" works well with third graders. Reading eight biographies is quite a chunk of reading for them, but having lunch with Santa is a strong motivation. Even the doubters get in the spirit of reading. Since your lunch will be in December, consider calling the local newspapers and television stations. At this time of year, photographers are looking for photos of Santa.

On the day you introduce the unit, pass out "Join the Biography Reader's Club" with the "Biography Reading List" copied on the backside. At the lunch, present copies of "Santa's Biography Reading Certificate." Don't forget to find someone to play Santa!

When you want to teach biography books at other times without a gimmick, use the half-sized sheet "Biography Books" and the more formal "Biography Reader" certificate.

Join the Biography Reader's Club and Have Lunch with Santa!

It's the time of the year to please your parents and yourself! Read! Read at least eight biography books between now and _____, and you will get to eat your lunch with Santa in the school library media center on _____. The two students who read the most will be Santa's helpers. Wow!

Don't miss out on this important event. Leave the cafeteria for a day and lunch with Santa in the wonderful library media café.

Sincerely,

School Library Media Specialist

Notes

1. Bring your own lunch. As you know, Santa is a little busy at this time of the year.

2. Complete the form on the back and turn it in BEFORE the day of the lunch.

3. Be prepared to meet with me and tell me about the books you read.

4. After you have read three books, you may write your name on the Biography Reader's Chart.

5. Aren't you glad you like to read?

Biography Reading List

Title	Date Read
1.	
2.	
3.	
4.	
5.	
6.	
7.	
8.	

I read these biography books.

Student Signature _____

My child read these books.

Parent Signature _____

Santa's Biography Reader Certificate

Awarded To

_____

For Reading Biography Books

Congratulations and Merry Christmas!

_____	_____
Santa Claus	Library Media Specialist
_____	_____
School	Date

Biography Books

Dear Students,

From now until _____, we will be studying biography books. You may read books from our library media center or the public library. (Some libraries use the letter B while others use the numbers 92 and 920 for biographies.)

If you read three biography books during this time, you'll receive a Biography Reader Certificate.

Please discuss the books with your parents, and when you finish, return this form to the media center.

Happy reading!

Library Media Specialist

I read these books:

1. _____
2. _____
3. _____

_____
Student Signature

_____
Parent Signature

Biography Books

Dear Students,

From now until _____, we will be studying biography books. You may read books from our library media center or the public library. (Some libraries use the letter B while others use the numbers 92 and 920 for biographies.)

If you read three biography books during this time, you'll receive a Biography Reader Certificate.

Please discuss the books with your parents, and when you finish, return this form to the media center.

Happy reading!

Library Media Specialist

I read these books:

1. _____
2. _____
3. _____

_____
Student Signature

_____
Parent Signature

Biography Reader Certificate

Presented To

_____

For Reading Biography Books

_____
Library Media Specialist

_____
School

_____
Date

CHAPTER 7

CALDECOTT BOOKS

In our school district, the library media specialists introduced the Caldecott books to second graders. Several of my friends held yearly Caldecott Float parades. Their students decorated shoeboxes representing their favorite Caldecotts and pulled them down the halls.

I never held a Caldecott Parade. For some reason, insect contests seemed fun but decorating shoeboxes didn't. Crazy, I know.

I usually spent six weeks on the Caldecott unit. First, I pulled the Caldecott books and shelved them together, and after we finished, I reshelved them. I never kept a permanent shelf of Caldecott or Newbery books. I wanted to encourage students to get in the habit of using every section of the library.

For the first lesson, I explained the Caldecott Medal Award Books and passed out the "Caldecott Reading Diary" and the "Caldecott Bibliography." Then, I showed the students a slide tape presentation of the books. I wrote and narrated the script on tape, and my students thought I was a movie star. Consider doing this yourself, perhaps on video. You can use it for several years, and it'll be a hit each time. If your Caldecott book display is mobbed and you have to referee a fight over a book, then know that your lesson was a success.

For subsequent lessons, I usually read the books to the students. Most of the second graders earned the award. I really wanted the parents to read the books to the children, but in years when I didn't have such parental support, I let the students count the books that I read to them.

On subsequent lessons, you can show commercially produced videos on the Caldecott books and illustrators. Watch the videos with your students; this is one of those subtle, powerful ways of reminding your students that they are important. To do your work while the students watch the video diminishes the lesson. If you absolutely must do something else, then apologize.

I have included two games—"Caldecott Puzzles" and "Caldecott Battle of the Books." Duplicate the pages on card stock, laminate them, and then cut them out. As a visual clue, use one color for the Caldecott games and another color for the Newbery games given in Chapter 12. On the back of each "Battle of the Books" question card, you may duplicate the name of the game on the back of the cards.

The purpose of "Caldecott Puzzles" is to match the title with the correct author and illustrator. On the back of the puzzles, copy the page that gives the year each book won the award. Make enough sets of puzzles so that students can work in pairs, and keep the sets in individual envelopes. This activity is quick, so you'll want to plan something else for your students to do when they finish.

"Battle of the Books" has been around for years, and there are a number of versions. In Arlington, Texas, the school library media specialists have designed a version for fourth and fifth grade students to: (1) read titles from a selected list of books, (2) try to earn a place on the school's Battle of the Books team, and (3) battle teams from other schools. District level winners receive trophies.

My version is not that complicated. On the day that you play the game, just divide the class into two teams by drawing an imaginary line down the middle of the class. You may want to let the students use their "Caldecott Medal Award Books" Bibliography.

Read a question aloud. Call on the students with the quickest hands—this is sometimes a judgment call. During the heat of the battle, you may have to remind your students that this is for fun. When you run out of cards, the game is over. It is not necessary to reward the winners with candy.

I did not make a game or puzzle question for every single Caldecott winner. I don't think it's necessary for students to know all of them. I used thirty of my favorite Caldecotts. Remember that "Reading Fun" is a homemade gift, tailored with my own personality. You may want to add some of your favorite titles, thereby reflecting your personality, too.

If I had it to do over again, I would do a Caldecott unit with the older students. An "official" unit would give them permission to enjoy the "baby" books. I'd let older students independently read a given number of Caldecotts, or I'd let them read aloud to younger students.

My Caldecott Reading Diary

Student —————————

Teacher —————————

About the Caldecott Award

The Caldecott Award is given yearly by the American Library Association to the illustrator of the most distinguished picture book published in the United States. The award is named in honor of Randolph Caldecott, a British illustrator who lived in the 1800s.

Dear Parents,

From now until ————————, we will be studying Caldecott Award books in the school library media center. A list of these books has been given to your child. Both the media center and the public library have many of these titles.

Students who read or hear eight books will receive a Caldecott Reader Certificate.

When you finish, please have your child return this diary to the school library media center.

Thank you for your help!

Sincerely,

School Library Media Specialist

Caldecott Reading Diary

I read or heard these Caldecott Books:

Title of Book	Date Read
1.	
2.	
3.	
4.	
5.	
6.	
7.	
8.	

Student Signature —————————

Parent Signature —————————

CALDECOTT MEDAL AWARD BOOKS

YEAR	TITLE	AUTHOR/ILLUSTRATOR
1938	ANIMALS OF THE BIBLE	Fish/Lathrop
1939	MEI LI	Handforth
1940	ABRAHAM LINCOLN	D'Aulaire
1941	THEY WERE STRONG AND GOOD	Lawson
1942	MAKE WAY FOR DUCKLINGS	McCloskey
1943	THE LITTLE HOUSE	Burton
1944	MANY MOONS	Thurber/Slodbodkin
1945	PRAYER FOR A CHILD	Field/Jones
1946	A ROOSTER CROWS	Petersham
1947	THE LITTLE ISLAND	MacDonald/Weisgard
1948	WHITE SNOW, BRIGHT SNOW	Tresselt/Duvoisin
1949	THE BIG SNOW	Hader
1950	SONG OF THE SWALLOWS	Politi
1951	THE EGG TREE	Milhous
1952	FINDERS KEEPERS	Will/Nicolas
1953	THE BIGGEST BEAR	Ward
1954	MADELINE'S RESCUE	Bemelmans
1955	CINDERELLA	Brown
1956	FROG WENT A-COURTIN'	Langstaff/Rojankovsky
1957	A TREE IS NICE	Udry/Simont
1958	TIME OF WONDER	McCloskey
1959	CHANTICLEER AND THE FOX	Cooney
1960	NINE DAYS TO CHRISTMAS	Ets
1961	BABOUSHKA AND THE THREE KINGS	Robbins/Sidjakov
1962	ONCE A MOUSE...	Brown
1963	THE SNOWY DAY	Keats
1964	WHERE THE WILD THINGS ARE	Sendak
1965	MAY I BRING A FRIEND?	de Regniers/Montresor
1966	ALWAYS ROOM FOR ONE MORE	Nic Leodhas/Hogrogian
1967	SAM, BANGS, AND MOONSHINE	Ness
1968	DRUMMER HOFF	Emberley/Emberley
1969	THE FOOL OF THE WORLD AND THE FLYING SHIP	Ransome/Shulevitz
1970	SYLVESTER AND THE MAGIC PEBBLE	Steig
1971	A STORY—A STORY: AN AFRICAN TALE	Haley
1972	ONE FINE DAY	Hogrogian
1973	THE FUNNY LITTLE WOMAN	Mosel/Lent
1974	DUFFY AND THE DEVIL	Zemach
1975	ARROW TO THE SUN	McDermott
1976	WHY MOSQUITOES BUZZ IN PEOPLE'S EARS	Aardema/Dillon
1977	ASHANTI TO ZULU	Musgrove/Dillon
1978	NOAH'S ARK	Spier
1979	THE GIRL WHO LOVED WILD HORSES	Goble
1980	OX-CART MAN	Hall/Cooney
1981	FABLES	Lobel
1982	JUMANJI	Van Allsburg
1983	SHADOW	Cendrars/Brown
1984	THE GLORIOUS FLIGHT	Provensen
1985	SAINT GEORGE AND THE DRAGON	Hodges/Hyman
1986	THE POLAR EXPRESS	Van Allsburg
1987	HEY, AL	Yorinks/Egielski
1988	OWL MOON	Yolen/Schoenherr
1989	SONG AND DANCE MAN	Ackerman/Gammell
1990	LON PO PO	Young
1991	BLACK AND WHITE	Macaulay
1992	TUESDAY	Wiesner
1993	MIRETTE ON THE HIGH WIRE	McCully
1994	GRANDFATHER'S JOURNEY	Say
1995	SMOKY NIGHT	Bunting/Diaz
1996	OFFICER BUCKLE AND GLORIA	Rathmann
1997	GOLEM	Wisniewski

Note: After you cut out each puzzle, be sure to cut between the title and author/illustrator.

Title	Author / Illustrator
Officer Buckle and Gloria	Peggy Rathmann

Title	Author / Illustrator
Smoky Night	Eve Bunting David Diaz

Title	Author / Illustrator
Grandfather's Journey	Allen Say

Title	Author / Illustrator
Mirette on the High Wire	Emily Arnold McCully

Title	Author / Illustrator
Tuesday	David Wiesner

Caldecott Winner
1996

Caldecott Winner
1996

Caldecott Winner
1995

Caldecott Winner
1995

Caldecott Winner
1994

Caldecott Winner
1994

Caldecott Winner
1993

Caldecott Winner
1993

Caldecott Winner
1992

Caldecott Winner
1992

Title	Author / Illustrator
Black and White	David Macaulay

Title	Author / Illustrator
Lon Po Po: A Red Riding Hood Story from China	Ed Young

Title	Author / Illustrator
Song and Dance Man	Karen Ackerman Stephen Gammell

Title	Author / Illustrator
Owl Moon	Jane Yolen John Schoenherr

Title	Author / Illustrator
Hey, Al	Arthur Yorinks Richard Egielski

Caldecott Winner
1991

Caldecott Winner
1991

Caldecott Winner
1990

Caldecott Winner
1990

Caldecott Winner
1989

Caldecott Winner
1989

Caldecott Winner
1988

Caldecott Winner
1988

Caldecott Winner
1987

Caldecott Winner
1987

Title	Author / Illustrator
The Polar Express	Chris Van Allsburg

Title	Author / Illustrator
Saint George and the Dragon	Margaret Hodges Trina Schart Hyman

Title	Author / Illustrator
Jumanji	Chris Van Allsburg

Title	Author / Illustrator
Fables	Arnold Lobel

Title	Author / Illustrator
The Girl Who Loved Wild Horses	Paul Goble

Caldecott Winner
1986

Caldecott Winner
1986
(Also 1982)

Caldecott Winner
1985

Caldecott Winner
1985

Caldecott Winner
1982

Caldecott Winner
1982
(Also 1986)

Caldecott Winner
1981

Caldecott Winner
1981

Caldecott Winner
1979

Caldecott Winner
1979

Title	Author / Illustrator
Noah's Ark	Peter Spier

Title	Author / Illustrator
Why Mosquitoes Buzz in People's Ears	Verna Aardema Leo & Diane Dillon

Title	Author / Illustrator
Arrow to the Sun	Gerald McDermott

Title	Author / Illustrator
The Funny Little Woman	Arlene Mosel Blair Lent

Title	Author / Illustrator
A Story—A Story: An African Tale	Gail E. Haley

Caldecott Winner
1978

Caldecott Winner
1978

Caldecott Winner
1976

Caldecott Winner
1976

Caldecott Winner
1975

Caldecott Winner
1975

Caldecott Winner
1973

Caldecott Winner
1973

Caldecott Winner
1971

Caldecott Winner
1971

Title	Author / Illustrator
Sylvester and the Magic Pebble	William Steig

Title	Author / Illustrator
Drummer Hoff	Barbara Emberley Ed Emberley

Title	Author / Illustrator
May I Bring a Friend?	Beatrice Schenk de Regniers Beni Montresor

Title	Author / Illustrator
Where the Wild Things Are	Maurice Sendak

Title	Author / Illustrator
The Snowy Day	Ezra Jack Keats

Caldecott Winner
1970

Caldecott Winner
1970

Caldecott Winner
1968

Caldecott Winner
1968

Caldecott Winner
1965

Caldecott Winner
1965

Caldecott Winner
1964

Caldecott Winner
1964

Caldecott Winner
1963

Caldecott Winner
1963

Title	Author / Illustrator
Madeline's Rescue	Ludwig Bemelmans

Title	Author / Illustrator
The Biggest Bear	Lynd Ward

Title	Author / Illustrator
Prayer for a Child	Rachel Field Elizabeth Orton Jones

Title	Author / Illustrator
The Little House	Virginia Lee Burton

Title	Author / Illustrator
Make Way for Ducklings	Robert McCloskey

Caldecott Winner
1954

Caldecott Winner
1954

Caldecott Winner
1953

Caldecott Winner
1953

Caldecott Winner
1945

Caldecott Winner
1945

Caldecott Winner
1943

Caldecott Winner
1943

Caldecott Winner
1942

Caldecott Winner
1942

Caldecott Battle of the Books

Caldecott Battle of the Books

Caldecott Battle of the Books

Caldecott Battle of the Books

In what book do two cats get lost during a fire?

Smoky Night

In what book does a girl help a famous tightrope performer?

Mirette on the High Wire

In what book does a dog help students with safety rules?

Officer Buckle and Gloria

In what book does a young man feel homesick for Japan when he is in America and feel homesick for America when he is in Japan?

Grandfather's Journey

In what book is there a boy, his parents, a train, and cows?

Black and White

In what book does a grandfather entertain his grandchildren?

Song and Dance Man

In what book do frogs float on lily pads?

Tuesday

In what book does a wolf try to trick three children?

Lon Po Po:
A Red Riding Hood Story from China

In what book does a man and his dog visit an island of birds?

Hey, Al

In what book do a princess and knight set off on an adventure?

Saint George and the Dragon

In what book does a girl and her father take a walk on a cold winter night?

Owl Moon

In what book does a boy lose a bell from his pocket?

The Polar Express

78

In what book are there short stories with morals and the characters include crocodiles, ducks, and lions?

Fables

In what book do animals escape a flood?

Noah's Ark

In what book do monkeys make a mess of the kitchen?

Jumanji

In what book does a girl get lost in a storm and join a herd of animals?

The Girl Who Loved Wild Horses

In what book does a boy search for his father?

Arrow to the Sun

In what book does Ananse try to trick the Sky God?

A Story—A Story: An African Tale

In what book does an iguana put sticks in his ears?

Why Mosquitoes Buzz in People's Ears

In what book does a woman make rice dumplings?

The Funny Little Woman

In what book does a battleground turn into a field of flowers?

Drummer Hoff

In what book does a boy get sent to bed without any supper?

Where the Wild Things Are

In what book does a donkey turn into a rock?

Sylvester and the Magic Pebble

In what book does a little boy visit the king and queen?

May I Bring a Friend?

In what book do twelve girls and a dog enjoy walks in Paris?

Madeline's Rescue

In what book does a girl give thanks at the end of the day?

Prayer for a Child

In what book does a boy put a snowball in his pocket to save?

The Snowy Day

In what book does an animal like maple sugar?

The Biggest Bear

In what book does a family of birds settle down in the Boston public garden?

Make Way for Ducklings

(Add your own question here.)

In what book does the quiet countryside grow into a busy city?

The Little House

(Add your own question here.)

Caldecott Reader Certificate

Presented To

_____

For Reading Caldecott Award Books

_____
Library Media Specialist

_____
School

_____
Date

CHAPTER 8

DEWEY DECIMAL PRACTICE

Whether the books with Dewey Decimal numbers are called nonfiction or informational books, your students need practice in finding them on the shelves. A room with thousands of books can be overwhelming. To become independent users of information, students need touchstones. That's why labeling your shelves is so important.

Label your shelves with the ten major divisions of the Dewey Decimal system and topics of interest to your students such as animals, drawing, jokes, and sports. You don't need cute little pictures. (To me, those sticky subject labels for book spines are messy and unnecessary.)

And don't bombard your students with worksheets on the Dewey Decimal System that they complete while sitting down, away from the shelves. The activities in this section must be completed by students who are on their feet and walking.

"A Hunt for Good Books" and "Nonfiction Books" work well with first and second graders. For "Nonfiction Books," cut out the pictures and attach them to your shelves, then remove them when the students are finished. Remember to permanently label your shelves with the subjects listed on the sheet.

Three activities for the older students are "The Ten Divisions of the Dewey Decimal System," "Favorite Numbers in the Dewey Decimal System," and "Exploring the Dewey Decimal System and Books."

I did not keep an easy nonfiction section because I wanted everybody to have access to information. There were times when older students needed books written simply and when younger students needed more detailed explanations. Our students could check out whatever they wanted, whenever they wanted. I never insisted that they must be able to read a book they checked out, and they certainly didn't have to keep the same books for an entire week. Students could come in every day, and if they wanted another book in ten minutes, they knew they could get something else. Choosing a good book takes practice.

My reasons for interfiling nonfiction books can be traced to Patsy Weeks, one of the most respected school library media specialists in Texas. For years, she ran a K-12 library media center in Bangs, a farm and ranch community. Patsy filed all fiction together and filed all nonfiction together. When other media specialists gasped, expressing fear that little children would make inappropriate selections, she explained that she trusted her students' judgment. Besides, she added, students could always return the book and get another.

Don't be too hasty in denying students access to certain areas of the library. Trust your students, and they will usually live up to your expectations.

Name _____   Date _____

A HUNT FOR GOOD BOOKS

We have good books in the school library media center! Find these sections in the nonfiction shelves and copy the symbol you see taped to the shelves.   Happy hunting!

Folk and Fairy Tales	Sports
Animals	Poetry

Name _____   Date _____

A HUNT FOR GOOD BOOKS

We have good books in the school library media center! Find these sections in the nonfiction shelves and copy the symbol you see taped to the shelves.   Happy hunting!

Folk and Fairy Tales	Sports
Animals	Poetry

87

Name _____   Date _____

Nonfiction Books

The school library media center has many good books. In the nonfiction section, you'll see these pictures taped to some of the shelves. Copy the number you find on the shelf label. The next time you want a good book, you can find it all by yourself!

_____

is the number for **Plants**

_____

is the number for **Music**

_____

is the number for **Dinosaurs**

_____

is the number for **Sports**

_____

is the number for **Animals**

_____

is the number for **Travel**

The Ten Divisions of the Dewey Decimal System

Nonfiction books are arranged by number according to the Dewey Decimal System. Go to the nonfiction shelves and find the ten major divisions. The names of the divisions will be on the shelf labels.

000 _____   500 _____

100 _____   600 _____

200 _____   700 _____

300 _____   800 _____

400 _____   900 _____

What section looks interesting to you? _____ The next time you go to the public library, practice the Dewey Decimal System.

The Ten Divisions of the Dewey Decimal System

Nonfiction books are arranged by number according to the Dewey Decimal System. Go to the nonfiction shelves and find the ten major divisions. The names of the divisions will be on the shelf labels.

000 _____   500 _____

100 _____   600 _____

200 _____   700 _____

300 _____   800 _____

400 _____   900 _____

What section looks interesting to you? _____ The next time you go to the public library, practice the Dewey Decimal System.

Favorite Numbers in the Dewey Decimal System

These numbers stand for certain subjects in the Dewey Decimal System. Find the following numbers on the bookshelves and write the subjects you see on the labels.

398.2 _____   636 _____

520 _____   743 _____

560 _____   796 _____

599 _____   817 _____

These are a few of the subjects you will find—Drawing, Fairy Tales, Jokes, and Sports.

Favorite Numbers in the Dewey Decimal System

These numbers stand for certain subjects in the Dewey Decimal System. Find the following numbers on the bookshelves and write the subjects you see on the labels.

398.2 _____   636 _____

520 _____   743 _____

560 _____   796 _____

599 _____   817 _____

These are a few of the subjects you will find—Drawing, Fairy Tales, Jokes, and Sports.

EXPLORING THE DEWEY DECIMAL SYSTEM AND BOOKS

The Dewey Decimal System has ten major divisions. Find these sections in the school library media center and examine the books. In each section, find one book you'd like to read and write the title, the author, and the call number.

000 GENERALITIES

100 PHILOSOPHY

200 RELIGION

300 SOCIAL SCIENCE

400 LANGUAGE

500 PURE SCIENCE

600 TECHNOLOGY

700 FINE ARTS

800 LITERATURE

900 HISTORY

CHAPTER 9

FAIRY TALES

Sometimes the silliest ideas are the most fun. One of our favorites was having lunch with the fairy godmother.

For years, I had just plain ignored the 398.2 section. Finally, with a push from my friend and library assistant Nancy McNiel, we spruced up the collection and came up with the idea of having lunch with the fairy godmother.

Third graders could have lunch with their fairy godmother if their parents read fifteen fairy tales with them. I wanted the parents to read the books so that the students could focus on the artwork and not struggle with long descriptive passages. Also, I wanted families to enjoy sharing books together, reminding parents of the importance of reading aloud—even when their children were big enough to read for themselves.

Since any older person can certainly read aloud—a grandparent, a godparent, or an older brother or sister—I've adapted the activity to give you that option.

This project lasted three weeks. Out of a hundred third graders, I usually had about thirty students who finished. Some years I skipped the fairy godmother and just promised the students a certificate and their name in the newspaper. This works, too, and while it's easier on your nerves, it's not as much fun.

Third graders really want to believe that they have a fairy godmother, even when their common sense tells them that they don't. I figure that a fairy godmother is someone who knows and cares for you and wants good things to happen to you. This could be only one person, of course, the assistant principal.

On the chosen lunch day, our assistant principal was ready. She wore a pink T-shirt plastered in glitter and a cheap, lined pink net skirt that I had made. I never had the heart to tell her that, as she paraded around the library, we could see right through that skirt.

We gave the students magic wands—glittered cardboard stars glued to popsicle sticks. If the students wanted, I put the barest amount of fairy dust (glitter) in their hair. Fairy dust, I reminded them, is powerful stuff (and tough to brush out.)

Some just ate their sandwiches and grinned. Other doubted. "This isn't a magic wand," they said. "It's a popsicle stick."

I shrugged. "Fairy godmothers are nice, not rich. They have to work with what they've got," I replied.

"That's not the fairy godmother," they continued. "That's the assistant principal."

"They do bear an uncanny resemblance," I said.

"And this isn't fairy dust. It's glitter," said the doubters.

"I guess you're right," I said. "The best magic comes from you and your own hopes and dreams."

The doubters would look up at me sort of squinty-eyed and, after a two-second pause, they'd ask for more glitter.

Join the Fairy Tale Reading Club & Meet Your Fairy Godmother!

Yes, it's true! If your parent or another older person reads fifteen fairy tales to you between now and _____, you will get to eat your lunch in the school library media center on _____.

You will also receive your very own magic wand and maybe even some magic fairy dust. What's more, the student who listens to the most fairy tales will get to sit beside the fairy godmother. **Wow!**

Join in the fun. Leave the cafeteria for a day and lunch in the fairyland library café.

Notes

1. Use the back of this sheet to record the books you heard.

2. Read books from the 398.2 section. This includes fairy tales, folktales, and tall tales.

3. Choose books with pretty pictures. You may choose books from our library media center or from the public library.

4. Be prepared to meet with me and tell me about the stories you've heard.

5. On the day of the party, bring your own lunch. Fairies are nice, not rich.

May You Make All Your Good Wishes Come True!

_____
School Library Media Specialist

My Fairy Tale Reading List

Book	Date Read
1.	
2.	
3.	
4.	
5.	
6.	
7.	
8.	
9.	
10.	
11.	
12.	
13.	
14.	
15.	

I read the above books to my child.

Parent (Or other older person) Signature: _____

After I heard each story, I retold it to the person who read it to me.

Student Signature: _____

Fairy Tale Reader Certificate

Awarded To

_____

For Reading and Listening to Fairy Tales

May You Make All Your
Good Wishes Come True!

_____ _____ _____
Your Fairy Godmother   School   Date

CHAPTER 10

INDEPENDENT SCHOLAR

At the end of school, we held an annual Award's Day, where students received a variety of awards. I decided we should have an Independent Scholar Award.

I wanted to offer smart students additional learning opportunities, as well as offering other students the same opportunities. I wanted an activity where students would independently take charge of their own learning. I also wanted students to begin thinking of themselves as scholars.

Every fall, I announced the award to the fourth, fifth, and sixth grade classes. I usually had some fifteen students who made the commitment. Many of the "scholars" were not our school's designated gifted students, and I think that standardized tests failed to recognize their talents—sheer tenacity.

I changed the requirements from year to year. Some years, the parents of these students and I would sit down and come up with things we wanted the students to experience. Requirements included activities such as writing stories or research papers, entering the spelling bee, presenting puppet plays, and, as always, reading.

I usually required two research papers. We went through all the steps: notes, outlines, bibliographies, rough drafts, final presentations. We worked after school or during recess. Of course, there were times when none of us wanted to do the work, but our commitment to each other kept us going.

For Awards Day, I bought each of the Independent Scholars a pin purchased from one of the library vendor catalogs.

I've included a sample contract for the Scholar Award. It's very basic. I've also included the book list that was the one requirement that never changed.

Independent Scholar Award

The Independent Scholar Award is given each year on Awards Day. The award is earned by fourth, fifth, and sixth grade students who pursue excellence.

To receive the award, students read at least forty books on a variety of topics. Students discuss their reading with their parents and with me. Students also write two research reports. Occasionally, the students miss recess or stay after school to meet with the other Independent Scholars.

Any student may pursue this award. It is challenging, of course. But here's hoping that you discover that learning is also rewarding.

Sincerely,

School Library Media Specialist

- -

Please return the contract by next week.

Student Contract for Independent Scholar Award

This year, I want to pursue the Independent Scholar Award. I will read the assigned books, write two reports, and meet with the other Independent Scholars. I have discussed the requirements with my parents, and they support my decision.

_____   _____
Student Signature   Parent Signature

_____   _____
Date   Date

NAME _____ DATE FINISHED _____

INDEPENDENT SCHOLAR AWARD
READING LIST

READ BOOKS FROM THESE SUBJECT AREAS. FOR EACH BOOK, WRITE THE AUTHOR'S LAST NAME, THE TITLE, AND THE DATE YOU FINISHED IT. TURN IN THIS LIST TO THE SCHOOL LIBRARY MEDIA SPECIALIST AT LEAST ONE WEEK PRIOR TO AWARDS DAY.

AUTHOR   TITLE   DATE READ

GENERALITIES 000-099, PHILOSOPHY 100-199, RELIGION 200-299

1. _____
2. _____

SOCIAL SCIENCE 300-399

3. _____
4. _____

LANGUAGE 400-499

5. _____

SCIENCE 500-599

6. _____
7. _____
8. _____
9. _____
10. _____

TECHNOLOGY 600-699

11. _____
12. _____

FINE ARTS 700-799

13. _____
14. _____
15. _____

LITERATURE 800-899

16. _____
17. _____

HISTORY 900-999

18.
19.
20.

BIOGRAPHY 92, 920 (OR B)

21.
22.

NEWBERY AWARD BOOKS

23.
24.
25.

FICTION BOOKS

26.
27.
28.
29.
30.

FREE CHOICE

31.
32.
33.
34.
35.
36.
37.
38.
39.
40.

ADDITIONAL READINGS

INDEPENDENT SCHOLAR
AWARD

Presented To

_____

For Outstanding Achievement in the Library Media Center

_____
Library Media Specialist

_____
School

_____
Date

CHAPTER 11

MYSTERY BOOKS

If you don't have a book on fingerprints, order one immediately. Our favorite was an old treasure—Robert H. Millimaki's *Fingerprint Detective,* published by Lippincott in 1973. Every spring, I started off the third grade mystery unit using Detective Millimaki's book. I showed the students the basic materials for a personal detective kit—a flashlight, a drinking glass, talcum powder, a soft brush, scotch tape, and black construction paper—professional materials, to be sure.

I asked some kid with sweaty hands (hot hands make better prints) to press his/her thumb on our glass door, whereupon I proceeded to brush the print with powder, carefully placing the tape over the print, and then transferring the tape to the black paper.

At this point, I had to do some fast talking because my evidence was more of a dusty mess than a print. "I'm a librarian," I'd say, "not an FBI guy. This is one thing you'll just have to practice on your own. And you'll get plenty of practice if you fingerprint your brothers and sisters. The next time they bother your stuff, don't argue with them, just fingerprint them, and take your proof to the judge, your mother."

In his book, Detective Milllimaki has a chart with the basic fingerprint types—the right-sloped loop, left-sloped loop, tented arch—and I had drawn them on a poster. We discussed the print types, and then I announced that I would fingerprint the class. "I'm not doing fingers," I'd say, "just one thumb. You can do your other digits at home."

As fast as possible, I grabbed a thumb, fingerprinted it, and announced in a detective voice, "Ah, a right-sloped loop." Or, "Ah, a left-sloped loop." And then in my teacher voice, "Go sit down."

As you can imagine, it's no easy feat running the computer and checking out books, fingerprinting thumbs, refereeing fights (because by now, the kids are hyper), and answering FBI questions all at once. But the first time you accomplish this without losing your sanity—well, you'll feel a little like Superman.

In this chapter, I've included two reading activities, a Mystery Reader Certificate, and a most official FBI Identification Card.

Mystery Reading Diary

Sh-h-h!

Dear Students,

From now until _____,
we will be studying mystery books in the school library
media center. Both the media center and the public
library have many mysteries for young readers.

If you read four mystery books during this time, you'll
receive a Mystery Reader Certificate. Just complete this
form, and return it to the library media center.

Sh-h-h! It's time for some mystery reading!

I read these books:

1.

2.

3.

4.

Student Signature:

Parent Signature:

MYSTERY BOOKS

Dear Students,

From now until _____, we will be studying mystery books in the school library media center. Both the media center and the public library have many mysteries for young readers.

If you read three mystery books during this time, you'll receive a Mystery Reader Certificate.

Just complete these steps: (1) read, (2) discuss the books with your parents, and (3) return this form to the media center. Have fun reading!

Sincerely,

Library Media Specialist

I READ THESE BOOKS:

1. _____

2. _____

3. _____

STUDENT SIGNATURE _____

PARENT SIGNATURE _____

MYSTERY BOOKS

Dear Students,

From now until _____, we will be studying mystery books in the school library media center. Both the media center and the public library have many mysteries for young readers.

If you read three mystery books during this time, you'll receive a Mystery Reader Certificate.

Just complete these steps: (1) read, (2) discuss the books with your parents, and (3) return this form to the media center. Have fun reading!

Sincerely,

Library Media Specialist

I READ THESE BOOKS:

1. _____

2. _____

3. _____

STUDENT SIGNATURE _____

PARENT SIGNATURE _____

FBI CARD

TOP SECRET

This official FBI Card (Fine Book Investigation) is to be used by all FBI agents under the age of twelve. This FBI Card is valid only if delivered by your school library media specialist. Void where prohibited.

FBI Board of Directors

The Chief
The Chief

GERONIMO
Geronimo

Bear Paw

School Library Media Specialist

FBI Special Agent Information

Full Name:

FBI Agent Signature:

Personal characteristics of FBI Special Agent:

Last FBI Activity (List some books you've read):

FBI Agent Thumbprint

On the inside of this card, give other important FBI information. (Use your imagination!)

108

Mystery Reader Certificate

Presented To

_____

For Reading Mystery Books

Library Media Specialist

School

Date

CHAPTER 12

NEWBERY BOOKS

I did a Newbery unit with fifth and sixth graders. At their age, many Newbery books are too difficult, both in the reading level and in the content. I did not want to spoil a good story by forcing it to be read too soon. My goal was to offer reading opportunities for the more sophisticated readers while giving average readers some background knowledge for use in future years.

My procedure for the Newbery unit was similar to the Caldecott unit. (See Chapter 7.) For the first lesson, I showed a homemade slide tape presentation and passed out a Newbery Reading Diary and Newbery Bibliography. Since reading certificates no longer seemed to motivate them, I used a free 100 coupon. Our sixth grade teacher, Nita McFarlin, designed the first one.

Before you pass out the Newbery Reading Diary, talk to your teachers about using the coupon in their classes. (See Chapter 4 for the coupon.) At our school, we let students use the coupon as a daily grade in their language arts classes, but we let them earn only one free 100. Several kids preferred reading to doing homework.

In case you have students who will work for an award, I've designed the Newbery Reader Certificate.

We enjoyed playing Newbery Bingo and Newbery Battle of the Books. Duplicate the games on card stock on a different color than the Caldecott activities.

Newbery Bingo is good practice for learning titles and authors. If you duplicate each of the nine different Bingo cards four times, you should have enough for a class set. If you want to add other titles, I've included a blank Newbery Bingo Card. Duplicate one set of the smaller cards, the ones with the authors' name. On the back, duplicate the "Newbery Bingo" sheet so that if a card gets misplaced, you'll know where it belongs.

To play, pass out the Bingo cards, the Newbery bibliographies, and some game chips. (You can buy chips or you can just tear up scraps of paper or poster board.) Using the smaller cards, read aloud the name of each Newbery author. Give the students time to find the corresponding title on their cards. The game is over when someone has a horizontal, vertical, or diagonal Bingo and calls out "Newbery Bingo!" Repeat the game as often as you like, but fifteen minutes of Bingo was usually my limit.

To play "Newbery Battle of the Books," divide the class into two teams by drawing an imaginary line down the middle of the class. Read a question aloud, and call on the student with the quickest hand. Students must answer with the correct title. As always, during the heat of the battle, you will have to remind your students that this is for fun. When you run out of questions, the game is over.

For these games, I did not use every single Newbery book. In a survey I conducted in 1996, some 2,000 sixth graders identified their favorite Newberys. When I designed these games for you, I used the sixth graders' top forty favorite books. You may want to add other titles.

For other lessons, you will want to show some of the commercially produced author videos. The videos on Beverly Cleary and Betsy Byars are old, but they are terrific. I've seen them so often that I believe I can quote them word for word.

Newbery Reading Diary

Dear Students,

From now until _____, we will be studying Newbery books in the school library media center. Both the media center and the public library have many of these titles.

If you read three Newbery books during this time, you'll receive a free 100 coupon that you may use in language arts class.

Just complete three steps: (1) read, (2) discuss the books with your parents, and (3) return this form to the media center. Happy reading!

Sincerely,

Library Media Specialist

I read these books:

1. _____

2. _____

3. _____

Student Signature: _____

Parent Signature: _____

Newbery Reading Diary

Dear Students,

From now until _____, we will be studying Newbery books in the school library media center. Both the media center and the public library have many of these titles.

If you read three Newbery books during this time, you'll receive a free 100 coupon that you may use in language arts class.

Just complete three steps: (1) read, (2) discuss the books with your parents, and (3) return this form to the media center. Happy reading!

Sincerely,

Library Media Specialist

I read these books:

1. _____

2. _____

3. _____

Student Signature: _____

Parent Signature: _____

NEWBERY MEDAL AWARD BOOKS

YEAR	TITLE	AUTHOR
1922	THE STORY OF MANKIND	Van Loon
1923	THE VOYAGES OF DOCTOR DOLITTLE	Lofting
1924	THE DARK FRIGATE	Hawes
1925	TALES FROM SILVER LANDS	Finger
1926	SHEN OF THE SEA	Chrisman
1927	SMOKEY, THE COW HORSE	James
1928	GAY-NECK	Mukerji
1929	THE TRUMPETER OF KRAKOW	Kelly
1930	HITTY, HER FIRST HUNDRED YEARS	Field
1931	THE CAT WHO WENT TO HEAVEN	Coatsworth
1932	WATERLESS MOUNTAIN	Armer
1933	YOUNG FU OF THE UPPER YANGTZE	Lewis
1934	INVINCIBLE LOUISA	Meigs
1935	DOBRY	Shannon
1936	CADDIE WOODLAWN	Brink
1937	ROLLER SKATES	Sawyer
1938	THE WHITE STAG	Seredy
1939	THIMBLE SUMMER	Enright
1940	DANIEL BOONE	Daugherty
1941	CALL IT COURAGE	Sperry
1942	THE MATCHLOCK GUN	Edmonds
1943	ADAM OF THE ROAD	Gray
1944	JOHNNY TREMAIN	Forbes
1945	RABBIT HILL	Lawson
1946	STRAWBERRY GIRL	Lenski
1947	MISS HICKORY	Bailey
1948	THE TWENTY-ONE BALLOONS	Du Bois
1949	KING OF THE WIND	Henry
1950	THE DOOR IN THE WALL	de Angeli
1951	AMOS FORTUNE, FREE MAN	Yates
1952	GINGER PYE	Estes
1953	SECRET OF THE ANDES	Clark
1954	...AND NOW MIGUEL	Krumgold
1955	THE WHEEL ON THE SCHOOL	DeJong
1956	CARRY ON, MR. BOWDITCH	Latham
1957	MIRACLES ON MAPLE HILL	Sorenson
1958	RIFLES FOR WATIE	Keith
1959	THE WITCH OF BLACKBIRD POND	Speare
1960	ONION JOHN	Krumgold
1961	ISLAND OF THE BLUE DOLPHINS	O'Dell
1962	THE BRONZE BOW	Speare
1963	A WRINKLE IN TIME	L'Engle
1964	IT'S LIKE THIS, CAT	Neville
1965	SHADOW OF A BULL	Wojciechowska
1966	I, JUAN DE PAREJA	de Treviño
1967	UP A ROAD SLOWLY	Hunt
1968	FROM THE MIXED-UP FILES OF MRS. BASIL E. FRANKWEILER	Konigsburg
1969	THE HIGH KING	Alexander
1970	SOUNDER	Armstrong
1971	SUMMER OF THE SWANS	Byars
1972	MRS. FRISBY AND THE RATS OF NIMH	O'Brien
1973	JULIE OF THE WOLVES	George
1974	THE SLAVE DANCER	Fox
1975	M.C. HIGGINS THE GREAT	Hamilton
1976	THE GREY KING	Cooper
1977	ROLL OF THUNDER, HEAR MY CRY	Taylor
1978	BRIDGE TO TERABITHIA	Paterson
1979	THE WESTING GAME	Raskin
1980	A GATHERING OF DAYS	Blos
1981	JACOB HAVE I LOVED	Paterson
1982	A VISIT TO WILLIAM BLAKE'S INN	Willard
1983	DICEY'S SONG	Voigt
1984	DEAR MR. HENSHAW	Cleary
1985	THE HERO AND THE CROWN	McGinley
1986	SARAH, PLAIN AND TALL	MacLachlan
1987	THE WHIPPING BOY	S. Fleischman
1988	LINCOLN	Freedman
1989	JOYFUL NOISE: POEMS FOR TWO VOICES	P. Fleischman
1990	NUMBER THE STARS	Lowry
1991	MANIAC MAGEE	Spinelli
1992	SHILOH	Naylor
1993	MISSING MAY	Rylant
1994	THE GIVER	Lowry
1995	WALK TWO MOONS	Creech
1996	THE MIDWIFE'S APPRENTICE	Cushman
1997	THE VIEW FROM SATURDAY	Konigsburg

NEWBERY BINGO

Lincoln	Missing May	FREE SPACE	Bridge to Terabithia
Call it Courage	Caddie Woodlawn	The Giver	The Voyages of Doctor Dolittle
The Midwife's Apprentice	Summer of the Swans	It's Like This, Cat	From the Mixed-Up Files of Mrs. Basil E. Frankweiler
The Bronze Bow	Sounder	Island of the Blue Dolphins	The Whipping Boy

115

NEWBERY BINGO

Joyful Noise	The High King	A Wrinkle in Time	Dicey's Song
Daniel Boone	FREE SPACE	The Matchlock Gun	Roller Skates
The Witch of Blackbird Pond	Invincible Louisa	King of the Wind	The Wheel on the School
Amos Fortune, Free Man	Hitty, Her First Hundred Years	The Westing Game	The Slave Dancer

NEWBERY BINGO

Up a Road Slowly	The Story of Mankind	Shiloh	Sarah, Plain and Tall
The Cat Who Went to Heaven	The Twenty-One Balloons	A Visit to William Blake's Inn	Maniac Magee
Jacob Have I Loved	Mrs. Frisby and the Rats of NIMH	FREE SPACE	Johnny Tremain
Rifles for Watie	The Grey King	A Gathering of Days	Walk Two Moons

NEWBERY BINGO

Dear Mr. Henshaw	Rabbit Hill	Julie of the Wolves	I, Juan de Pareja
Number the Stars	Mrs. Frisby and the Rats of NIMH	Sarah, Plain and Tall	Shiloh
Bridge to Terabithia	Summer of the Swans	The Wheel on the School	King of the Wind
Up a Road Slowly	FREE SPACE	The Midwife's Apprentice	Invincible Louisa

NEWBERY BINGO

A Wrinkle in Time	The Giver	Shiloh	Maniac Magee
From the Mixed-Up Files of Mrs. Basil E. Frankweiler	Island of the Blue Dolphins	The Whipping Boy	Sounder
The Slave Dancer	Call It Courage	Rifles for Watie	The Grey King
The Matchlock Gun	FREE SPACE	Amos Fortune, Free Man	The High King

NEWBERY BINGO

Missing May	The Story of Mankind	It's Like This, Cat	A Gathering of Days
Lincoln	Number the Stars	The Witch of Blackbird Pond	A Visit to William Blake's Inn
Walk Two Moons	FREE SPACE	Roller Skates	The Twenty-One Balloons
Daniel Boone	Hitty, Her First Hundred Years	Dicey's Song	The Voyages of Dr. Dolittle

NEWBERY BINGO

Shiloh	Bridge to Terabithia	Island of the Blue Dolphins	The Bronze Bow
Sarah, Plain and Tall	FREE SPACE	Dicey's Song	The Giver
The Midwife's Apprentice	Summer of the Swans	Rabbit Hill	Dear Mr. Henshaw
Caddie Woodlawn	Joyful Noise	Mrs. Frisby and the Rats of NIMH	The Westing Game

NEWBERY BINGO

The Cat Who Went to Heaven	FREE SPACE	Johnny Tremain	Jacob Have I Loved
The Grey King	The Twenty-One Balloons	Call it Courage	I, Juan de Pareja
The Witch of Blackbird Pond	The Matchlock Gun	Dear Mr. Henshaw	A Gathering of Days
Sounder	Caddie Woodlawn	Amos Fortune, Free Man	The Voyages of Dr. Dolittle

122

NEWBERY BINGO

Walk Two Moons	Maniac Magee	Number the Stars	FREE SPACE
Joyful Noise	A Wrinkle in Time	Missing May	Lincoln
Julie of the Wolves	The Whipping Boy	The High King	The Westing Game
King of the Wind	Mrs. Frisby and the Rats of NIMH	From the Mixed-Up Files of Mrs. Basil E. Frankweiler	Rabbit Hill

NEWBERY BINGO

Newbery Bingo

Newbery Bingo

Newbery Bingo

Newbery Bingo

Newbery Bingo

Newbery Bingo

Newbery Bingo

Newbery Bingo

Karen Cushman

The Midwife's Apprentice
1996

Sharon Creech

Walk Two Moons
1995

Lois Lowry

The Giver - 1994
Number the Stars - 1990

Cynthia Rylant

Missing May
1993

Phyllis Reynolds Naylor

Shiloh
1992

Jerry Spinelli

Maniac Magee
1991

Paul Fleischman

Joyful Noise
1989

Russell Freedman

Lincoln: A Photobiography
1988

Sid Fleischman

The Whipping Boy
1987

Patricia MacLachlan

Sarah, Plain and Tall
1986

Beverly Cleary

Dear Mr. Henshaw
1984

Cynthia Voigt

Dicey's Song
1983

Nancy Willard

A Visit to William Blake's Inn
1982

Katherine Paterson

Jacob Have I Loved - 1981
Bridge to Terabithia - 1978

Joan Blos

A Gathering of Days
1980

Ellen Raskin

The Westing Game
1979

Susan Cooper

The Grey King
1976

Paula Fox

The Slave Dancer
1974

Jean Craighead George

Julie of the Wolves
1973

Robert C. O'Brien

Mrs. Frisby and the Rats of NIMH
1972

Betsy Byars

Summer of the Swans
1971

William Armstrong

Sounder
1970

Lloyd Alexander

The High King
1969

E.L. Konigsburg

*From the Mixed-Up Files of Mrs.
Basil E. Frankweiler - 1968
The View from Saturday - 1997*

Irene Hunt

Up A Road Slowly
1967

Elizabeth Borton de Treviño

I, Juan de Pareja
1966

Emily Neville

It's Like This, Cat
1964

Madeleine L'Engle

A Wrinkle in Time
1963

Elizabeth Speare

The Bronze Bow - 1962
The Witch of Blackbird Pond - 1959

Scott O'Dell

Island of the Blue Dolphins
1961

Harold Keith

Rifles for Watie
1958

Meindert DeJong

The Wheel on the School
1955

Elizabeth Yates

Amos Fortune, Free Man
1951

Marguerite Henry

King of the Wind
1949

William Pène Du Bois

The Twenty-One Balloons
1948

Robert Lawson

Rabbit Hill
1945

Esther Forbes

Johnny Tremain
1944

Walter Edmonds

The Matchlock Gun
1942

Armstrong Sperry

Call It Courage
1941

James Daugherty

Daniel Boone
1940

Ruth Sawyer

Roller Skates
1937

Carol Ryrie Brink

Caddie Woodlawn
1936

Cornelia Meigs

*Invincible Louisa: The Story of the
Author of Little Women*
1934

Elizabeth Coatsworth

The Cat Who Went to Heaven
1931

Rachel Field

Hitty, Her First Hundred Years
1930

Hugh Lofting

The Voyages of Doctor Dolittle
1923

Hendrik Willem van Loon

The Story of Mankind
1922

Newbery Battle of the Books

Newbery Battle of the Books

Newbery Battle of the Books

Newbery Battle of the Books

In what book does a girl travel to Idaho in search of her mother?

Walk Two Moons

In what book does a man make beautiful whirligigs?

Missing May

In what book is there a girl named Dung Beetle?

The Midwife's Apprentice

In what book does the word *released* have an unusual meaning?

The Giver

In what book does a boy who likes to run become a legend?

Maniac Magee

In what book is there a love poem about two book lice?

Joyful Noise: Poems for Two Voices

In what book does a boy hide a beagle dog that he has found?

Shiloh

In what book does a girl try to save her friend from German Nazis?

Number the Stars

In what book is there a boy named Prince Brat?

The Whipping Boy

In what book does a boy put an alarm on his lunch box?

Dear Mr. Henshaw

In what book does a poor boy grow up to be one of the most photographed men in American history?

Lincoln: A Photobiography

In what book is there a cat named Seal and a woman who loves the sea?

Sarah, Plain and Tall

In what book do you find poems for innocent and experienced travelers?

A Visit to William Blake's Inn

In what book does a girl describe her life on the family farm in New Hampshire?

A Gathering of Days: A New England Girl's Journal

In what book do children live with their grandmother because their mother is in a mental institution?

Dicey's Song

In what book do you read about twin sisters growing up on an island in the Chesapeake Bay?

Jacob Have I Loved

In what book do a boy and a girl create a magical kingdom in the woods?

Bridge to Terabithia

In what book is a young boy kidnapped from New Orleans and ordered to play his fife on a ship?

The Slave Dancer

In what book do sixteen people try to solve a mystery and inherit a fortune?

The Westing Game

In what book is there a strange Welsh boy named Bran?

The Grey King

In what book does a widowed mother mouse try to get her family to safety?

Mrs. Frisby and the Rats of NIMH

In what book does a dog that has been shot crawl under the cabin?

Sounder

In what book is a girl lost in the Alaskan wilderness?

Julie of the Wolves

In what book does a girl search for her retarded brother Charlie?

Summer of the Swans

In what book do a brother and a sister run away to the Metropolitan Museum of Art?

From the Mixed-Up Files of Mrs. Basil E. Frankweiler

In what book does the pet of a New York City boy jump out of the car window?

It's Like This, Cat

In what book is there an assistant pig keeper named Taran?

The High King

In what book does a black slave boy named Juan become friends with a Spanish painter?

I, Juan de Pareja

In what book are a sister and a brother left alone on an island?

Island of the Blue Dolphins

In what book does a girl leave her home in the Caribbean to live in a stern Puritan community in Connecticut?

The Witch of Blackbird Pond

In what book do three children go to a strange planet by traveling in an unusual way?

A Wrinkle in Time

In what book does a boy act as a spy during the Civil War?

Rifles for Watie

In what book does a professor who is tired of teaching math decide to take a trip?

The Twenty-One Balloons

In what book does a young boy take part in the Boston Tea Party?

Johnny Tremain

In what book does a slave in the 1700s earn his freedom?

Amos Fortune, Free Man

In what book do animals look forward to people moving into the big house?

Rabbit Hill

In what book is Mafatu afraid of the sea?

Call It Courage

In what book does the author tell the history of the world?

The Story of Mankind

In what book does a boy protect his family from Indians in the early days before New York was a state?

The Matchlock Gun

In what book does a Wisconsin tomboy miss a dog named Nero?

Caddie Woodlawn

Newbery Reader Certificate

Awarded To

_____

For Reading Newbery Award Books

Library Media Specialist

School

Date

CHAPTER 13

SUMMER READING CALENDAR

The summer reading calendar was one of our favorite activities. Every fall, a few weeks after school had started, we held a pizza party for the kids who had read for thirty minutes or more each day during the summer. We'd turn out the lights, use candles, and serve our students in the library media "café." One time a student said, "Hey, with the lights out, you can't see the dust on the shelves." That line showed up in my book *38 Weeks till Summer Vacation,* when Nora Jean and the gang have pizza at school.

At the end of the school year, I passed out the reading calendars to the third, fourth, and fifth graders. (I tried this idea with the younger students, but I didn't feel it was as successful.) In my teacher voice, I would announce that I was passing out their summer homework. On cue, I'd first get groans, then grins. I always reminded them that if they missed a day of reading, they could read more on the next day.

One year, I included a list of recommended books. Even though I clearly stated that these were suggestions and that the public librarian would have other good ideas, the parents and kids focused only on the books on the list. I never provided another bibliography as I wanted the students to take initiative in discovering books and to get some individualized help from the public librarian.

Notice that the dates are missing on the summer reading calendar. You'll need to type them in each year.

Summer Reading Fun

June

Sun	Mon	Tues	Wed	Thu	Fri	Sat

July

Sun	Mon	Tues	Wed	Thu	Fri	Sat

August

Sun	Mon	Tues	Wed	Thu	Fri	Sat

Dear Students,

Want to make this the best summer ever? Want to explore the world and not have to leave your backyard? Want to tickle your funny bone?

Then join in the fun! Read for thirty minutes or more each day. You may read books, magazines, or newspapers. It even counts if your parents or other older persons read to you. Ask the public librarian for some good book suggestions, and find out about their summer reading program.

Once you have read thirty minutes or more, cross out that day on the calendar. When school starts in the fall, drop your calendar by the school library center. You will earn a Summer Reader Certificate and a party! That's right. Every student who completes the calendar earns a party!

Make this the best summer ever. **READ!** Encourage your friends to read. And get ready to party!

Sincerely,

Summer Reader Certificate

Awarded To

_____

For Reading During Summer Vacation!

Library Media Specialist

School

Date

ABOUT THE AUTHOR

For many years, Mona Kerby served as the library media specialist at J.B. Little Elementary School in Arlington, Texas. Now she is an assistant professor and graduate coordinator of the school library media program at Western Maryland College in Westminster, Maryland.

She is an award-winning author of children's books. Two of her books, *Asthma* and *Cockroaches,* were named to the 1989 Outstanding List of Science Trade Books for Children. In 1994, *38 Weeks till Summer Vacation* received the Maud Hart Lovelace Award.

In 1997, Kerby created "The Author Corner," a web site for students in the middle grades (3–8) to meet Mid-Atlantic authors and illustrators of children's books.